Antiepithalamia
& Other Poems of Regret and Resentment

————

JOHN TOTTENHAM

PENNY-ANTE | EDITIONS

PUBLISHER	Penny-Ante Editions PO Box 691578 Los Angeles CA 90069 United States of America *penny-ante.net*
ISBN	978-0-9855085-2-4
CATALOGUE NO.	PA-009
COPYRIGHT	2012 by Penny-Ante Editions *All rights reserved, including the right of reproduction in whole or in part. Except for private study, research, criticism or reviews, no part of this book may be reproduced without prior written permission. Inquiries should be made to the publisher.*
COVER IMAGE	John Tottenham: *Twilight in Sweetheart Lane* (2010)
BOOK DESIGN	Rebekah Weikel
MISC.	Printed in Iceland

I

Antiepithalamia

ANTIEPITHALAMIUM I

At last, their smugness is united:
their compatible vacuity,
their insufferable beaming.
They were meant for each other,
to the exclusion
of all other possibilities,
all other meaning.

A woman with a past meets a man
with no future.
He exchanges his celibatarian pallor
for her placid beige face,
upon which tremulously reigns
expectation of adoration
and relief from the responsibilities
of a life without boundaries.
All in the name of love,
as if it were some moral drug.
Something definite
to agonize about.
A thankless task:
this radiance
in which you bask.

This is exactly what we always craved:
permission to collapse
into pointless struggle,
to plunge greedily
into the possessive pronoun.
To speak,
as we have always wanted to speak:
in the first person plural.

You pined for suffocation, freedom
to immerse yourself
until all else faded
into indifference.
For too long you were the center
of nobody's universe.
Now you are my doorknob,
you are my earthworm, you are my lover.
A bleeding heart on a stick:
caring more about 'us' than anyone else
or each other.

ANTIEPITHALAMIUM II

Congratulations, you found a wife.
A spouse is not hard to find.
Most people are looking for one.
So why wouldn't you?
You followed the dream
down a one-way street
to a dead-end.
It gave you something to do.

You are the one:
the one who will save me
by putting up with me,
more through process of elimination
than affinity. The one
I've been waiting for,
as nurse, jailer and whore;
the secret of my failure;
a tortoise demanding lettuce
at my door. But, above all,
what I love most about you
is the way that you love me,
although my spirits tend to contract
in such close proximity, and shrivel
into distance. Be that as it may,
what kind of fiend would choose
to live without such a necessity?

Why do you want a wife?
Does a kettle sustain
the shrill intensity of its whistle
indefinitely? This self-centered selflessness
requires a closed system in which to thrive.
But you'll never get out of the world
entwined. An emptier freedom awaits you,
that leaves no room for doubt:
a shelter for the weary, a dream
you can live without.

& Other Poems of Regret and Resentment

ANTIEPITHALAMIUM III

The only thing I don't like about sex
is the intimacy. And the only thing
I don't like about intimacy
is the isolation it calls forth,
the elicitation of needs
that otherwise remain unbidden
but now demand to be surfeited.
A stifling craving created
by transfusion, submersion
into some slow moving river or the tides
of the moon, supposedly. Or petals
shooting out of stems like blood
red raindrops
on a rose, the flower
from which all the burdens fell.

In this lonely new world of secret harmonies
and sudden dissonance, a greedy enslavement
to sensation turns desire into a demand,
a necessity. A sudden deadness
accompanies satisfaction,
and nothing else
satisfies.

It was all so much sweeter
when you were relatively indifferent.
Now everything else pales by comparison.
Nothing holds you anymore.
Other diversions have all lost their savor
and receded, because you tried to drink the ocean
when a glass of water was all you needed.

ANTIEPITHALAMIUM IV

One's powers of conviction or calculation
are called upon to nurture the conceit
that one is never going to find another
who possesses the singular compatibility
of one's mate,
and if such another does exist,
they will be resisted
in favor of a mutually enriching form
of self-deprivation:
a junction or a termination
of one's options, or admission
that one has none. A gauge
by which one measures emptiness;
the only drop of sweetness
in an otherwise bottomless existence.

Craving captivity, tentatively,
we weigh our needs,
what it is that we both want:
the same thing, hopefully,
that everybody else wants;
and whether we are likely to get it
by making a shrewd investment
in one another's future.

We blossom in deadlock
afterglow, an unavoidable affinity
dictated by time and propinquity,
secure at last in the knowledge
that only the shared kind of happiness
truly matters in this life.

How liberating it is
to restrict oneself,
to make a choice
and adhere to it,
and how courageous:
to open oneself up
to this newly defined world
of protected borders
and a conclusive center.

It was worth all the sacrifices,
the dereliction of desires,
the letting go of the old
and other ways.
It was the best thing you ever did.
You discovered something
more important than yourself:
the person you chose
to become a part of you,
and, of course, the fruit
of that union, a combination
of the two.

You are the most important thing
in my life. I want you
so that nobody else can have you.
Not like I have you,
as keeper of the key
to what I want
to need and need
to believe in,
as living proof
of my existence.

Involvement with another person
does take away from involvement with oneself,
and that, of course, is selfless:
There are now two of you to selfishly consider.
You share the same values, trusting
in a security that is more valuable
than anything else.
Because nothing could be worse
than lacking it.
And if it should fade,
of what then would you be made?

ANTIEPITHALAMIUM V

I always assume that people I admire are single,
and experience a sinking sensation
when I learn they are not. They drop
in my estimation (for what that's worth)
from wishful thinking to cold hard earth.
Until this unpleasant disclosure I had optimistically assumed
they were alone... in the world:
the state in which they entered and will leave
(so why not elect for a reprieve?)
Now they become suspect; their choice seems cold-blooded,
a defect, suggestive of a questionable integrity
and a lack of purity, a defection: they gave up, surrendered
to the obvious, to something they wanted to feel,
in order to justify cutting a deal.

Was it just fear
of being excluded or unwanted,
did you think that you had somehow failed,
that your life was not complete?
Was it only through not being alone
that you could be made whole,
that made you submit, as if it were some singular feat,
to 'an insidious form of social control'?

It must be a comfort to have somebody special.
A fact, obviously, so relentlessly is it enforced
in story and song, celebrating the apparent sacred truth
that nothing else in the world is as important
as the abiding affection of the one whom one has chosen
to validate one's existence. As if there were nothing else to sing of.
Two people loved each other: So what? These things happen.
As do other things.

Convenient, is it not,
that two hearts so often beat as one?
Such a happy coincidence
that the one you have chosen to give yourself to
feels the same way about you.
You have decided to accept each other.
It beats the alternatives.
And after the pleasure: a state of exposure,
of suspension, a love that grows
in direct proportion to fear;
a prolonged tension
that sharpens into staleness,
into a way of passing through life.

It all seems quite pointless.
As does being alone.

PLEASANTVILLE

Entering into a relationship is like moving to a small town.
A new beginning, a way of saying 'this is the end, it's over,
I give up.' You have had enough. Those numbered days,
throughout which everything spun, are numbed.
That dizzy season of distraction and receptivity
couldn't last: It took too much out of you. Your sense
of wonder is now exclusively reserved for the exploration
of a new world that barely exists outside yourself.

But small towns contain a certain boring beauty
that occasionally bores into you.
They are slower, cleaner, safer places: ideal for retirement.
And it is comforting to know
that one's neighbors share the same position,
the same priorities, the same sense of belonging.

The entire world will become one room
in one town. And nothing of interest lies beyond the city limits.
It's all right, you didn't want to go out anyway.
Other people and their breeding habits
no longer hold any fascination.
It was time to move beyond sensation, free
from the inconveniences of a world wide-open,
into an idyllic dormancy,
muddying temptation with connubiality.

Bells ring across the fields each passing hour,
covering just the right amount of distance
for those hard-won moments of tranquility
to flower. You found what you were searching for:
somebody to fill a void - as a squirrel fills a void -
in a place of refuge, taking its form from the land.
Mating for life, behind closed doors,
in a bungalow built just for two.
Even the good times are boring.
But they will come back to haunt you.

& Other Poems of Regret and Resentment

ANTIEPITHALAMIUM VII

I always find it comforting
when I hear of couples separating.
It gives me a lift.
It seems to confirm
the natural order of impermanence.
Despite dutifully practicing those courtesies
vital to the sustaining of a union,
despite all the material proofs,
despite all the 'work' that was put into it,
it belied its original promise.
And didn't last forever.

How strange to find you were not a couple after all.
You only wanted to be comfortable;
it didn't seem like too much to ask for.
For to love connubiality is to love life:
this is how the race perpetuates itself,
through a contract between a woman and a man,
like a job that you love,
with profit sharing and a pension plan.

A laborious process:
this accumulation of unconditional love.
The security, of course, makes it all worthwhile:
the pleasure of having something other than oneself
to morbidly worry about. For it is difficult,
to the point of pointlessness, to live without love
and the promise of it in return.

We enter into it at first
with the attitude of two people
who want something from each other
and are nice about it.
Finally, nothing else matters anymore
(strange that anything else ever mattered before).
We were stumbling around in the darkness,
but now we can focus on what we have always wanted
to focus on: the most important thing in life:
this mutual decision to remain together
in one place and face each other
over thousands of meals,
with nothing to say,
saying it anyway,
day after day.

I think of you
not as another person
but as another dimension of myself.
In much the same way that I think of our child
and our property. My love has imbued you
with a fatal vulnerability: my own vulnerability.
And we will be together even after we die.
Anything less would be an insult to each other
and an affront to eternity. But when one person wants out,
the other has to comply. And sometimes
we have to care enough to release each other
into a newfound freedom, never more urgently alive
than when infused with fresh hate. How bracing it is
to find that we don't really need each other. Then again,
one can always find somebody else. Why wait?

II

In my preterminal days, on my way to cipherhood.

SONG OF DAWN

I saw the sun rise by accident.
It was a horrible sight.
Annoyed by its splendor,
I sought refuge in a moist pillow,
and lay there, alone,
at the dawn of another day,
that brought me closer to death,
pondering the vanity of my solitude,
the vanity of procrastination,
and the tiresome inevitability
of waking up again the same person.
It might still be possible to change,
but obstinately I remain the same,
hoping that others might take solace
in my consistency.
But perhaps they take no solace in it,
perhaps they too find it tedious.

SPRINGTIME IN AN AMERICAN TOWN

Why is it that I only ever notice my gut in motel room mirrors?
Perhaps obesity is contagious in these parts,
the natural result of pride and fear.
And why am I not noticed here?
Barely branded by sidelong glances
in one dead-eyed town after another
by a populace whose chief talent lies in the ability
to instantly distrust anything they don't understand.
The feeling is mutual.
I have passed like a ghost through your cities,
scavenging for scraps of the past.
I have rambled, ambled, bled your cities dry,
arriving at the end of the trail of trash,
weighed down on the great white way,
on tired streets of dead blood-red brick.
And I have found the old buildings,
in all their purity,
perfectly preserved, in paint,
on the sides of new buildings,
in towns like silences
that need not be filled.
And there is nothing left anywhere
that hasn't been turned over
and undermined by overawareness.
For in this tarnished day and age,
the luster of everything must be restored
and celebrated with meat and sugar,
and a soundtrack of feigned emotion.

There's a lot of ugly laughter in this world:
stranded in other people's reality,
trapped by freedom and vexed
by pointless innovations
in a homogeneity somehow born
of distance and inconsistency.
Discovering myself again
as a useless member of society:
belonging nowhere, only wishing
I wasn't wishing
I wasn't here.
Meditating, amid ruins,
upon the ruin of myself,
realizing that the decline of all I hold dear
can be traced to the moment
that I first became
aware.

AVALANCHE

I am the stale receptor, the superfluous accumulator,
the redundant completist trapped in his cave of musty retention,
buried under years of absorption... unaborted,
decades of consumption... consumed,
sacrificed at the altar of other people's art,
while everything else fell apart.
Pondering, at last, all the pointless consolation,
questioning if it was really necessary to devour entire genres
until I was crapulous from gorging myself on culture,
As if it were some kind of achievement
to accumulate all this knowledge that will die with me.
So that on my headstone it will read: that I read
and lived a lot of fiction... that Art ruined my Life.

A MATTER OF HONOR

Eventually one went too far
in not going far enough.
Purely for the satisfaction of knowing
conclusively, that one had been true to oneself,
at the expense of oneself.
A matter of honor: to have left nothing
and never changed, to have sustained oneself
only on private moments and pretend acclaim.

Sad
that it was all so ill-used: Time
that was deliberately squandered,
merely to enhance regret,
while incessantly bemoaning
the lack of discipline: that was a sort of discipline,
and the choice: not to make a choice,
to endlessly prematurely celebrate one's downfall
until it became irreversible.

A few years of such abnegation
would have been plenty;
one didn't have to drag it out
for a quarter of a century:
making sacrifices,
based on fallacies,
that nobody noticed,
negating every possibility
until one was left with nothing
but integrity, and a slowly surfacing urgency
that must now be sacrificed to necessity.

LANDSCAPE WITH PEASANTS

The footsteps of bored guards echo in the empty galleries.
A homeless patron wheels a laundry cart around.
Despite free admission, the place is empty,
these are the only sounds, and it's easy to get lost
in the bleak, rural Dutch 17th century.

Beneath a cloudy, unforgiving sky,
two figures tramp down a muddy lane
toward a house half-hidden behind gnarled trees.
Cattle graze beside a river.
Beyond torn fencing fields recede.

Gazing into these serenely battered bygone scenes,
one is reminded of real life, real weather:
that it might still be out there somewhere.
Not here, far removed from European culture,
at the very edge of the western hemisphere.

Where, on a hollow, cloudless day
the collection's fragile incongruity is quickly wiped away
by the umpteenth oblivious jogger running by
with a head set on.

There's nothing in the air.
The sun, subtly vampiric, brushes against a world
where everything and nothing is in bloom:
a seductive vacuity, of lifeless trees
and lives of ease and loud complacency,
as soothing and beautiful as a cartoon.

PASSING WIND, PASSING WATER

Casting a long shadow upon a lonely trail,
I pause and pass water, watching it stream
into the shape of an umbilical cord
or tornado funnel. Pockets of warm wind
cradle canyon corners. Here there is only silence,
emptiness and regret, something like life
after death; a claustrophobic reeling,
a time alone that comes of nothing
and of nothing is revealing.
The cries of raptors merge with the cries of prey,
becoming one long scream of pain, madness
and pleasure that fades into a pulsating silence,
from which emerges a train whistle
from indeterminable tracks, unknown terminal.
While the lava flow of night traffic pours
into a dying shade of blue.

RECIPISCENCE

I scaled the dizzying heights of negation,
and looked down, dismissively, upon stability.
I bragged about discomfort, fostered the illusion
of disillusion, and resented the success of friends.
Such a position, eventually, became hard to defend.
It was lonely and boring, the air was too thin,
I had to descend. Out of the faded clouds of glory,
to find that what was once perversity was now reality,
and the fiery idealism of youth a rank steam rising
from a pile of wet rags. Soaked through, never wrung out.
Led to gravel by a trail of gold. A long way down,
while I put myself on hold.

LIT LIFE

Learn to be obscure. Otherwise you're done for.
Leave them something to do. Or they'll think less of you.
The idea is to make it appear that something's there,
to make you struggle to discover that nothing's being said,
and nothing's being read. The fathomable is anathema,
the decipherable unutterable, a curse. What could be worse
than being understood? To be referential is to claim validity,
a means of being taken seriously. But does anyone really care
who 'the hyacinth girl' was? Would it make any difference
if you knew her/his identity?

& Other Poems of Regret and Resentment 35

SUICIDAL HIT PARADE

In the hierarchy of suicided poets,
Plath is Number One, secure in her position,
with pillowed head in oven.
No poet will ever be that famous again,
such a salve to other people's pain, but not her own.
Number Two, not without a trace, not like a stone -
With a thud on a frozen river, John Berryman.
Number Three, flung into warmer waters -
lost at sea, among other places - Hart Crane.
Further down, by the fountain, dying of thirst,
the Lysol drinkers - Charlotte Mew: "I am sorry to say I am";
and Vachel Lindsay: "They tried to get me, I got them first."
Broken by being broke. Remove the v and switch the t,
and poverty is poetry. Trakl, too much coke;
Celan, another poet overboard; Kleist, just bored to death,
after sixteen cups of coffee; Jarrell, a one hit blunder;
Sara Teasdale, who shouldn't have cared, cared enough to die.
Those who drank from a poisoned chalice: Sexton, Chatterton.
And other long lost lives, losing the thread they were hanging by:
Anna Wickham, a long walk off a short chair.
Nerval, from a window grating on a black and white night.
Or, in the Roman style, with a bowl of warm water,
a new razor blade and a smile. Beware the irreversible gesture.
Frank Stanford, heartlessly, with three bullets to the heart -
posthumously peaking, he continues moving up the chart.
And those, like Marc Penka, whose names other poets
sometimes stumble on. And recent entries, carrying on
the rich tradition: Sarah Hannah, Rachel Wetzsteon.
Suicide is a dying craze in the world of poetry:
the patina of tragedy enhances a legacy,
capping a lifelong brush with obscurity.

III

*I have a heart like a wheelbarrow;
there are no windmills in my mind.*

PEARLS BEFORE SUNRISE

Your need of me has awoken a need in me.
I enjoy the attention. I am attracted
to the attraction. I have tried to defuse, demystify
and humanize you. I have sought out your imperfections
and I have found them. I have stared
at the hair on your arms and the protuberances
on your back. The incipient stubble on your legs
reminds me of my mother. But none of this
matters. You have selectively directed your femininity -
knowing, intuitively or otherwise, that the gift is yours
to bestow and withdraw as you see fit - and in doing so,
you have shown perfect taste.

We lie side by side, basking in the warm glow
of an attraction tempered by considerations
of age and failure. The window of opportunity narrows
as irresolution asserts itself.
Perhaps you would be offended, puzzled
and disgusted by such an intrusion.
It might be asking too much of anybody:
to stanch this thirst, no longer sweet,
and dwindling into hesitation.

Maybe it's just cowardice.
Or simply unwillingness
to drag others into this mess.
The descent seems predetermined,
a decision close to self-deceit.
I appreciate the appreciation.
But must one engage? Let's dispense
with the preliminaries, cut straight
to the defeat.

That you have grasped my essence
makes you vulnerable, avoidable,
even ugly. I cannot help but notice
how easily food gets stuck between your teeth,
and stays there.
And that your teeth are discolored… stained.
And please refrain from smiling
during the act of darkness:
This is not a cheerful occasion.

Leave me to long
for no one in particular, to retire
from this realm of delight, and return
to the stasis I hold dear: these are words
that no one wants to hear.

A profound connection was established:
You recognized my worth;
you gave me something I wanted,
even in the midst of dearth. I was grateful.
I was able to be myself around you. And that
was something that couldn't be. It might have been
exalted… exhausted… forget it. I liked myself better
the previous impression you had of me.

PRICKSAND

When bodies merge and melt together,
an attachment, naturally, is formed,
of which one wishes to be the sole recipient.
After enough familiarity one begins to experience
the sensations of the other party and enter,
through the body, another's mind,
almost as if it were your own body.
It is almost as if you didn't exist,
as if neither of you exist,
as if nothing else exists.
You take it personally
and you wonder how it feels
for the other party.

I will love you more
if you let me hurt you.
Your readiness to endure my pain
creates a disheartening closeness
that I would rather live without.
But if deprived of it, I will want it again.
Until this sweetness, never free
and usually painful, finally dries up.

I cannot bear the thought
of anybody, other than myself,
hurting you. And nobody else
can be allowed to satisfy you.
Not until I no longer care what you do,
or with whom. Such speculations
are exhausting: the birth of boredom,
conceived in aphrodisiac jealousy.
The need to duplicate pleasure
is the source of much misery
in this world.

We became, on occasion, one:
hence this sundered feeling.
Imagining you as a dull memory, an absence
of unnecessary needs, coming into focus
as you recede; a passing pain, attached to a name.
No longer a friend, just somebody else's end.

Well, it was time to move on, anyway:
the beauty wasn't in the consistency.
Still, it is hard to look back upon that misalliance,
among other misalliances, without the usual regrets,
without ruing that there were other things
I should have been doing.
Not that almost everything doesn't produce that effect.
But you could at least wave, you left waste.
Or how about one last hate fuck.
For old time's sake.

THE REAL THING

Whenever I'm in a relationship
I feel as if I'm being unfaithful
to myself.
I long for the day
when my longing
will dull.
It is only a matter of taking it,
of putting it in:
the time
that must be filled,
drifting between (and during) fixes,
emerging from afterglow haze
into further craving;
creating boredom, a vacuum
in which insecurity flourishes;
and dragging myself to the bar of judgement
for the slightest blunder or betrayal
of a system that I never believed in.
But this is no forum in which
to measure one's worth,
only a need
that feeds upon itself
needlessly.
And what have I learned
from all these affairs of the heart?
One thing only, and that
what I knew to begin with:
that I have no business being in one at all.
The endless interlacings of strategy and pining
amounted to nothing more
than a cheap source of whining,
and what is now most welcome is the absence
of anticipation, of dragging out a dream
beyond its natural duration,
into a predictable chaos of whispers
and screams that nobody else,
hopefully, will ever hear.

It is painful
to find it's not painful,
soon diminished, forgotten, unclear:
an efflorescence
indistinguishable from erosion,
both acetylene and anodyne;
a great squandering of emotion,
it flattens and fades,
congealing into precious waste.
How quickly love, for want
of a better word,
turns to distaste.

DESIRE AND DESIRABILITY

I am tired
of looking at every woman I encounter
as if she embodied redemption or deliverance
from my apparent incompleteness.
As if, left to my own devices,
I am somehow impure, irrelevant,
or simply outnumbered.

I can already taste the emptiness
she'll bring.
Less lodestone than tombstone:
Digging into her
like a man digging his own grave,
towards an uncertain grail.
Not an anxiously awaited goal
but a gift,
only furtively thirsted for,
that must be endured,
acknowledged or honored
if it presents itself: a mere pause
between states of insufficiency.

My heart swells
at the prospect of being desired
by someone desirable.
A certain burden of tenderness
is laid in reserve for such occasions:
bottlenecked and squirming,
sometimes leaking out,
and taking a long time to mop up.
Another party is required as catalyst
to recreate something that already exists,
that becomes septic and stale
when denied release.

This other party
is poorly rewarded for their participation.
Never mind, they fulfilled their task.
And upon sober reflection, perhaps
they were not worthy of the honor after all.
All the mystery covered up the fact
that there was nothing
to conceal. Another reminder
that only the fleeting connections
and missed opportunities are real.

INAPPETENCE

Upon those increasingly rare occasions
when I am faced with a willing woman,
I see only future pain, an invitation
to unhappy pleasure, and soft wind
after the rain.

Queasiness, apathy and doom
spread over the sweetness: fear
of the stagnation and sorrow
that will have to seep out, fresh
from the source, all that death,
dirt and hurt. Better for it to be absorbed
than apprehended, but who could withstand
such a force? A rallying call to weakness,
better leave it hanging.
But dread is soon replaced by regret,
indifference by longing.

But to touch something, knowing that it is not foreign,
that it will not shrink from one's need or intent:
that also would become tiresome.

So we bide our time in hesitation,
our bodies trailing our minds.
There is something in the air,
or somewhere, that requires definition,
but your touch might dissolve
in such mere physicality. An empty beckoning
sealed with a kiss from between gritted teeth
that turns into a sneer. No darkness,
depth, warmth or mystery there.
It should never have been left to linger.

COUPLES AT PARTIES

Why do couples always appear tired together at parties?
Was the process of 'finding' each other so exhausting
that they now need to take a long rest?
Or is it because they're bored of each other?
Or are they worn out from the effort of pretending
to be interested in anything other than each other?
Being charming with strangers seems quite pointless
at this point. It is draining maintaining
this front: She's hardly there at all.
She sits on his lap, yawning.
She feels sorry for you
because you can't have her.
And she distrusts you because your hungers are not accounted for.
While he seems distant but content, happy with his 'choice.'
Holding her hand signifies his priority,
and it will remain held on the drive home,
their reserves finally unflowing, as they give voice
to sympathy for those unfortunates who do not have
what they have.

A LOVER'S PLEA

I know I'm not making this proposal
with the correct amount of charm,
rejection has already been factored into my tone of voice, but....
Might you be amenable to my ministrations?
I have thought about you while masturbating. I long to see you
in a pose of squashed supplication. I want you
to want to give me pleasure. I want you to be satisfied
by my satisfaction. I am excited by the thought
of your being excited by me. Please understand
that these feelings you inspire in me
are a tribute to your qualities. I would be flattered
were you to entertain the possibility of letting my love
set you free.

TENSE OFFERING

Perceive and recoil, I understand,
the burden of my need is too naked,
and it borders upon other even less acceptable states,
tightly wound but quaking. It hints of doom
and therefore is doomed; the body cannot lie
and neither can my intonations: trying to hide the hunger
only makes it more awkwardly visible, killing any chance
of reciprocation. The implausibility of your assent
is the only hope of reconfiguration. But it would
be asking too much, even from somebody who claims
to understand. I cannot affect the indifferent touch
necessary to assume command. I cannot pretend
to be in control of my gratitude. I am too potentially
painfully grateful. And where would such gratitude lead,
what would it unleash, for how long would it remain pure?
Please continue to disregard me. It's better that way.
Forget I was ever on the verge of doing anything.
It would be too much for either of us to endure.

IV

*Itching to trump you with a finer whine:
One of superior bitterness.*

REGRETS

I don't understand people
who claim that they have no regrets in life -
who insist, out of gratitude, pride or ignorance,
that they wouldn't want to change a thing.
My life is a raging river of regret, flowing
into a sea of shame. There is very little
I wouldn't do differently if given a second chance.
I always knew I'd end up feeling this way:
It was a setup. Regret was something
I worked towards, something I felt I had to earn.
And now, naturally, I regret that too.

SUMMERTIME IN A EUROPEAN CITY

What am I doing here, in this soft transparency,
staring into the mysterious flow of traffic,
apathetically? Appetite is an afterthought,
and summertime is something worth waiting for: to dissolve
in a disturbing lack of tension, a luxuriously grueling boredom
in which both worries and contentment lack conviction.
The metallic shiver of sunlight in the leaves
evokes a bygone world of pain,
unscathed by lust, which, in an older culture is surprisingly neither
richer or deeper than elsewhere else. Still, it is refreshing
to have a new place to complain about.

PARTY TIME

Why do people walk away from me at parties?
They have asked me nothing but they have detected
that something is missing, that doesn't fit
into their scheme of things. They lack curiosity
but their other senses are still sharp: lack
of the right kind of politely controlled hunger
is soon smelled out, as is lack of money.
When I am shunned, I imagine it is because I am doomed.
My lack of sense of self has been gauged;
my self-made rootlessness has been grasped.
There is something not quite right about me.
But before I have even confessed
that there is absolutely nothing going on in my life,
my potential interlocutor has prepared his method of escape:
It involves a trip to the bar. It is understood
that 'excuse me, I need another drink' is code for
'you have nothing to offer me.'
When put on the spot,
the riches of my life trickle into vacancy.
The dreaded question is dealt: What do you do?
And how do you know so-and-so? Such facts
must first be established if we are to move on to other things.
But I have already flunked my opportunity to be interesting.
To be upbeat all the time is not only boring, it is exhausting:
born of dearth of genuine enthusiasm, subconscious whoring.
And it is only the absence of a shared motivating force
that creates this social chasm: this roomful of awkward silences
filled with awkward speech, where we hover over the buffet
and attempt to look indifferent
to the food we shovel onto our plates.
Old friendships are renewed: 'What about old Nick?' –
'Didn't you hear, he got married.' – ' I'm sorry,
I didn't know he was sick.' People-watching is engaged in
as an emetic. And behind a costly smile, a flaming softness:
another notch on the old wilting broom handle or a deepening
flatness. You could have had her. But you adhered to a policy
of destructive ambiguity, resulting in a broken window
of opportunity. You didn't pounce, she fled, leaving you
alone with the unseized moment. But that's all right:
you can go home and masturbate about her instead.

ROCK ON

You chose me to be the soundtrack to your life
and for that you will worship me and live forever
in suspended adolescence: a face in the crowd, mesmerized
by the spectacle of other people enjoying themselves;
staring at a stage upon which eccentricity is legitimized
and awkwardness magically transformed into allure;
lost in somebody else's dream, feeding off their potency,
downstream.

Women enjoy the company of musicians
because they harness musical form to sexual energy:
conventional rebels in their uniforms of studied casualness;
Heroes because in-between 'struggling' with substances,
they produced a few good songs.

The mistake was in thinking there was any connection
between reality and this tired celebration of second-hand sin:
A pose that dissolves beyond the boundaries of a system
that is now designed to suck you in, to saturate with dilution
the lifestyle choice of succeeding generations
disproportionately drawn to the same line of self-expression.
The entire enterprise is exhausted but supply meets demand,
and there's always more than enough to go around.

SCORCHED EARTH POLICY

Bitterness is all the rage.
Resentment burns through me,
destroying everything in its path;
burning up the sadness, burning up regret,
burning up fear and desire;
charring, gutting, exhausting me.
I can't take the corrosive bitterness
I have forced upon myself.
I know that it's all my own fault.
But I can't let that stop me
from resenting other people.

ARTISTS ANONYMOUS

Because I wasn't born
black or poor or talented,
I waged a private war
publicly. I contrived my vices by proxy
and watched myself as I paid my dues,
striving to struggle, searching
for something to lose. Insecurity
became my pathway - a short cut
to credibility - a way to earn immunity
from hope and fear: the right to weep openly
and hold hands unashamedly
over coffee, cigarettes and prayer.

PARASITOLOGY

How infinitely rich and rewarding my life has been.
How vast in its depth and diversity has been my delight
in absorbing other people's work.
How diligently I have kept myself to the task
of studying every root and branch
in numerous fields of the arts,
instead of honing my own craft.

I measure my life by other people's milestones.
All this evasion, absorption and accumulation
provides a foundation in tradition,
a rich vein of consolation.
Art, like death, makes life more interesting.
And without it: as unthinkable as love
without pity, or a selfless eulogy.
But the bondage of receptivity
compares most unfavorably
with the selflessness of productivity.

Without it, how much emptier but looser life would be.
Time would become untracked, there would be less looking back.
Without it, I might have been grateful and valued simplicity,
might have had definite goals, a destiny I could control -
instead of ceaselessly indulging my curiosity;
an insatiate craving for something to relate to;
a hunger verging upon greed: Out of loneliness
and laziness we reach out to those
who reach into themselves
out of need.

WOODSHEDDING

Grooming myself for a career in failure,
I studied with masters.
Then I realized: they were successful.
For how would they otherwise be known?
There is a difference between the failures
of the successful and the failure of true failures.
A matter of sliding scale:
The failures of the successful are celebrated,
broadcast far and wide,
while the failures of failures are obscure,
buried with them when they die.

LOOSE ANGELS / LOST ANGLES

Above these yellow streets, in searing sunlight,
beautiful women brandish guns, delivering the message:
death is fun, and life is cheap...
and you're all suckers, lined up like sheep.
The poison pours out of here: 'the dream factory,'
where the sanctioned dreams are assembled,
the fantasies designed to soften minds, the little
that the little people are allowed to enjoy.
We come here, eager to be sucked into the system, grateful
to surrender to the triumph of attitude, the death of the will;
to make our contribution to keeping things at a standstill.

Did you really think that you would never tire of palm trees,
that a presence, once consoling in its pointlessness,
might not become oppressive; that you might not tire
of the sun's sullen mockery, its mad refusal to decay,
and end up envying reality,
beyond this cocoon of numbing warmth,
this once necessary softness turned stale?
For it can be easy to forget, in this shallow slumber,
that when your numbered days are numbed,
your numb days are still numbered.

OF OR RELATING TO

No matter how much proof
of having enriched other people's lives,
you're still not satisfied: you must persist
in tirelessly yielding the gift that is only yours to give.
Imagine you hadn't given it: unthinkable
for us. How empty our lives would be.
We went on this journey with you,
sharing your joys and sorrows
from a respectful distance,
but without the accompanying surges
of carefree glory and securely bittersweet sadness.
Such sensations were out of reach, impractical, awkward.
But that's all right: We just enjoyed your life instead.

And your reward for having given of yourself:
to keep giving. Never mind that you dried up
long ago. Why let that stop you?
And to actually enjoy life: strange concept,
but you earned it, and you don't really
have anything better to do.

Behind all the trappings, naturally,
you are far from content.
All the freedom that money can buy
and all the love that art can supply
can't keep the demons away.
You were happier when you were scuffling.
How can that be?
With the woman who is beautiful enough
to understand you and your children three:
surely that provides an airtight legacy.
And when you die, a little bit of the world
will die a little with you.
Is that not sufficient compensation
for the humiliation of mortality?

I could have had your golden life,
of course, had I wanted it badly enough.
But it seemed more interesting, at the time,
to sell myself short. I was at liberty
to deprive myself. And now I am free
to begrudge success.

While you were busy making your name,
passionately committed to the Idea,
I didn't understand that it was just an excuse
to have a career.
The doors that kept opening for you
are the same doors that kept closing on me.
Still, it provides consolation
to know that the fullness of your satisfaction
lacks the purity, depth and ripeness
of the brief flashes of happiness
that I occasionally experience.

NATURAL BEAUTY

If this really is the last of life
that I am far from savoring,
why am I still wavering?
Why not just get it over with?
It seems as good a time as any.

The foliage rustles
with a soothing morbidity,
while trees are distant and aloof,
as if aware of my fate
but requiring proof.

Nature has given up on me
and beauty is my enemy.
I sought it out and found it
where it didn't belong.
Now it elicits difficult memories
and it's just gone.

V

From elationship to disintegrationship.

LOVE STORY

I cannot locate the source of the disturbance
that has blossomed between us.
It seems, possibly, real... untranslatable.
At best it can be mumbled incoherently,
requiring a different language:
one that you can only feel.
And a different form of currency,
in which I lack sufficient means.

Nevertheless, a situation has arisen
that demands my complete attention:
You persevered beyond the numbness,
even after your jaw cramped, to induce
a state of constant sickly anticipation
of something sweet: an impatience to wallow again
in a mutually tacit sense of wonder, to swoon
into a different kind of loneliness,
from which I restlessly await recovery
and the long snarled return to a serene apathy.

FIRST BLUSH

My future seems bleaker than usual today.
The sun is tired, the streets are dead,
and those who walk upon them appear
more menacing and alien than before.
It all compares most unfavorably
with our time together.
Your sweetness embitters familiar scenes;
your softness makes everything else harder.
You have given me something new: an emptiness
that can now only be filled by your presence,
a solitude that never before seemed threatening.
Did you bring it with you or was it already there?
I can't tell, and I can't tell
anybody else, for fear of inviting ridicule.
And I can't tell you, for fear of repelling you,
and because I don't trust myself
to maintain interest
once these initial convulsions have subsided.

SECOND BLUSH

I felt a pang, an aberration.
Stasis pierced, an insidious elation.
You are lost to me now:
your strange simplicities
and slate blank stares, dissolved
in a blur of fixation.

And I am lost to myself.
I resent you for bringing out these feelings:
I was better off without them.
You have evicted me from myself,
banished me to a semi-autonomous region,
to a statelessness beclouded
by fear of regret.

Now that you're around, there is less of me
to go around. I don't like myself
as much as I used to. And other people
don't seem to like me as much either.
I used to spread my want among many,
and nobody noticed it. Now you get it all,
and you notice it.
It isn't much of a bargain:
to get less of every other aspect of my life
in exchange for more of the one thing
that strips me of my identity.

I don't feel empty within myself,
I feel empty without myself.
We were supposed
to be in the same place
but we couldn't be
much further apart.
You don't seem to be experiencing
the same discomfort that I am experiencing,
and I resent you for that also.
You have no idea how I'm feeling,
and I'd like to keep it that way.

But hiding one's feelings all the time is hard work.
You have touched me deeply and you must be touched
deeply, striking a massive gusher of anxiety
once enough softness has been penetrated.
A rich vein of insecurity: it exhausts itself
eventually, and pipelines are laid in place
to another world of waiting
for boredom, and then of postponing pain
while prolonging boredom.

DISAMBIGUATION

When you are with me, a tree is not a tree.
Or not as much of one as it used to be.
Many things are no longer what they once were:
what I grew used to, that grew used to me.
Everything is hazy now: distant, muted, depleted
of purity. You overshadow other solaces
with the gift that you inconsiderately bring.
I experience an acute sense of separation
from myself. Even solitude, when it can still be embraced,
becomes muffled, unedged, almost alien.
I'm hardly there anymore, and won't reappear
until I have finally driven you to drive me from your door.

How easily one gets sucked
into these ill-considered arrangements,
halfheartedly attempting to make something permanent
out of a fleeting remedial lapse.
Maybe it should be accepted, even if it is unwanted.
After all, it is a gift, wrapped in expectation
and filled with hopelessness: a delicately dull grind.
Just give up, let go,
let the low hanging fruit die on the vine,
and leave the leaves waving in the wind,
timeless and true.
And this, because it isn't timeless,
doesn't mean it is any less precious
than the amount of time
that has been spent resisting it.

& Other Poems of Regret and Resentment

FUTURE WIFE

Your beauty shines through the prism of my guilt,
melting into tenderness. I can't breathe
without that precious boredom, that sweet suffocation.
But the burden of beauty is that it must be sullied.
To sour such lethal sweetness is irresistible.
Restlessness returns, boredom becomes tawdry,
and you break it until you can't take it
anymore. It is fun to hurt the one you love.
Much more fun, obviously, than hurting somebody
you don't care about. Patience must be tested.
A proof of love, if they can take it. If not,
then they're weak and they don't care enough about you.
And as they withdraw, you crave the softness
that you never craved before.

IRON ANNIVERSARY

The object of this restlessness that puzzles you
is solitude: a loneliness for loneliness,
a wistfulness for restlessness,
a straining back to what comes naturally –
the way things used to be
when I had only me.

I miss myself madly.
I long to be romantically involved
with myself again, like old times:
dependent only upon independence,
demanding only temptation.
I'm better off in an empty kennel,
unmuzzled and free:
that was the essence
of my doghouse epiphany.

Upon your encroachment my world shrinks.
My energy level sinks. I feel as if I'm fading away.
But your need of me is addictive: It keeps me warm,
the way a tea cozy maintains the pot's warmth
long after the tea has lost its flavor.
Now I am continually both parched and sated,
sapped, tired of feeling, halfheartedly clinging.
With or without you my life has no meaning.

& Other Poems of Regret and Resentment

THE ARTIST'S WIFE

How empty your life must be without me,
without anybody
to blanket with caresses
and otherwise oppress with tenderness.

Your sadistic kindness was occasionally repaid
with masochistic asperity. It was enough, apparently,
for you to assume that you would always be wanted,
to continue undaunted: looking up at me occasionally
as a dog gnawing on a bone looks up at an approaching stranger.

My way of giving was to let you give.
But that initial torrent of generosity soon dried up,
leaving scant evidence of that which briefly flowed between us:
a meniscus of drool fading on the edge of the sofa,
a mouth full of dust, and the distant echoes
of a form of impassioned utterance
turned toward an end I never had in mind.

I might have missed you more if you had missed me less.
And I might have missed myself less.
Your attentions sadden me. I dread summertime:
The sight of you in a summer dress.
The idea of collaboration has never interested me.

CONSTANCY

I look back with great shame upon my infidelities,
mortified by my inability to have fully enjoyed them.
What was my problem, where was the illicit thrill?
I was hardly even there, all it did was make me ill.
Even with that one from the health food store,
who told me to do whatever I wanted to do to her.
And I did nothing.

What folly: How I chastise myself now.
Even when I could easily get away with it,
it made me uneasy. I felt guilty,
as if I shouldn't want to slide my hand
down the back of a pair of jeans, across a new ass.
I dreaded all the deception, the exhausting anticipation
of discovery. It seemed like too much work.
I had to pass.

Monogamy, I have long suspected, is a scam:
a deviation practiced by the pedestrian,
like jaywalking, a law that I have no respect for.
Yet I stand there respectfully, restlessly,
waiting for the light to change,
while others walk straight into traffic with impunity.

Is it a source of strength or a weakness
to fail to be satisfied by compromise,
a bargain or a sacrifice: to watch
the wasted opportunities slip by?
Since you have become my conscience,
temptation has become poisonous.
A game of inches, unsustainable.
I can't hope to survive
on the sly.

It would hurt too much to hurt you
and to taste the resentment that rejection
of the gift would inevitably bring.
Lust crushed by sympathy, shattering
the simplicity. Either way,
I couldn't stray. I starve the need,
greed, or something in-between,
and resent myself, and you,
accordingly.

A YEAR SINCE SUNDAY

Funny, isn't it, what stirs
one's sense of wonder:
A sparrow on the window sill,
a weed growing through a crack in the sidewalk,
a raindrop on a rose,
a tree swaying in the wind,
or your tongue sliding over my perineum.
I marvel to think that such beauty is capable
of penetrating what's left of my life.
Just when it seemed dead,
it was reawakened
by the sensitizing impurity of your touch.

It's altogether too much.
I am dazzled by the precocity of your elegance
and taste, your irreproachable shamelessness,
the unadorned intricacy of your rape fantasies,
and your essential moral core.
I'd hate to see it go to waste.
Most of my time is spent
resisting crying out for more,
reigniting memories that fill the day
with holes, bringing me closer
to a situation beyond my control.

Having emptied myself, the emptiness deepens
into a warm glow, out of which longing flows.
Unintended acceleration dulls the mind,
fixing the details on freeze and rewind:
an endless cycle of replay and repeat
that leaves the rest of my life incomplete.

A few of the few thousand nights of your youth
provide fuel, consolation and proof:
the exposed stains on the mattress
where the sheet tore loose,
the pillow where your head lay buried,
moaning sour blasphemies by candlelight,
the tender cruelties and vicious calculated thrusts,
the linen spattered with memories,
the scent of cloying lust.

Cold, hard, incandescent,
it all feels right:
a form of focus, a frame, everything falls
into place. But soon enough,
enough is not enough:
the frame gets bent, the focus
gets blurry. If I could only see you again,
it might dull these pangs for an hour or two.
If that... maybe not.
Either way, please hurry.

ENCHANTMENT

My mental processes used to surprise and delight me.
Now they nauseate me.
All I think about is you.
The dispassionate appraisal of subtle abstractions
supplanted by the parsing of our every trifling interaction.

I've never felt this way before
since I felt this way before.
In your absence, I'm absent.
Wanting you, everything else is wanting.
On those rare occasions that I catch myself
not missing you, I miss missing you.
I remember peacefulness, I remember other things
that preceded and will succeed you.
Dazed between stations, time slowly dies:
something to be killed between assignations.

MY LAST SPURT

A disembodied voice reminds me
that it's all about the body:
a pleasing distance, an advance.
The body reminds me that I have no choice,
that I don't stand a chance.

When I see you something comes over me,
a sort of mystical lust.
My feelings get involved,
insofar as lust can be described
as a feeling. It triggers other feelings
that must be contained, sustained or killed.

At first you feel like nothing
in my arms, flimsy and wicked.
Assuming purity and substance
as you melt beneath me.
Every stroke counts,
as if it were the last one.
As if truth were embodied in those thrusts,
or an alluring deceit, hinged upon
and fueling the conceit
that something profound flows between us.

A case, then, of simply resigning oneself
to the fact that it's just sex, as if that isn't enough.
It summons other stuff: all that messy emotion.
Love or whatever it's called.
Making it, creating it
out of gratitude and greed.
Getting off on you getting off on me...
or somebody else. An exercise in mutual vanity.
This death, as opposed to my other deaths,
feels dangerously like spring.
A catastrophic waste of time,
but I wouldn't trade it for anything.

VI

*The rest is gravy:
gravy in the rain.*

SERIOUSLY

The time has finally come
to take myself seriously.
But I don't have the energy.

Sometimes I have to pause to consider
my lack of progress, my lack of gratitude,
my lack of moral vitality, my vital forces in decline.
But it's a little too late for that. I never drew a line
between a man of property and a beggar on horseback.
An imperative of blithe disaffection always held me
back: a superstitious adherence to the truth, some sort
of fidelity. What I take most seriously
is that I shouldn't take myself seriously.

Oppressed by shallow strivers, I hid my light.
I waited too long, until it was gone,
ignoring my potential, stuck in the experiential,
under siege and in flight.

Because other people took themselves too seriously
I didn't take myself seriously.
Enough.

CREDIT AND CREDIBILITY

Wait, there must be some sort of a mistake.
This isn't how my life was supposed to turn out.
Things haven't worked out the way I planned,
because I didn't work, because I didn't plan.
I stacked the deck against myself
and played the self-dealt hand.
It shouldn't have been surprising
when it came up thin.
As any sucker knows,
scared money never wins.
The denial's part of the deal.
But still, it seemed unfair
that a seat wasn't being reserved for me
at the big table, that I found myself
paying a mysterious debt to a nonexistent creditor,
and wanting credit for what I imagined
I could have done.

ARTISTS ONLY

Never mind that you have nothing to bring to the table.
No problem, that is no longer a requirement.
A career in the arts is no longer the province of the unlucky few
who did what they had to do. Like poker, it's a game open
to everybody now, and the tables are crowded with players
hungry for easy money and televised prestige.
Sacrifices are demanded of those who waver, hesitation is fatal;
false modesty or self-doubt get you quickly shaken out.
But the quality of the game has become vitiated, impenetrable
to the uninitiated, and the less talent you possess,
the more brazenly it must be heralded. Lay a golden egg
where carelessness meets calculation. The artist's touch:
It pays, these days, to advertise your desperation.

NIGHT OF THE LONG SMILES

I see you seeing through me,
projecting and magnifying your fear onto me,
recoiling as you would from the sight of a corpse
that is still pungent with the scent of failure.

Your gut reaction is to flee, but we're trapped
and must endure certain formalities.
Throughout which ordeal, between strained utterances,
you turn slowly, painfully, almost imperceptibly away,
until your back is entirely facing me, and finally,
with great relief, I can walk away.

Perhaps it unnerves you to assume
I'm unaware of the impression I make upon you.
Or perhaps what makes you uneasier is your awareness
of my own uneasy awareness of my apparent condition.
Either way, a brief exchange of civilities should suffice.

It isn't nice to feel
that you have to avoid eye contact with somebody:
to avert an aversion and honor an awkward unspoken pact,
because they have made it so obvious that your presence
makes them uncomfortable. It is disappointing
disappointing disappointing people.

PILGRIMAGE

Snow falls outside the hotel window,
floating carelessly through the air...
and I don't care.
The town spreads out below me:
A sprawling red-brick dream,
with white capped peaks beyond.
But I don't respond.
Crushing boredom, grueling emptiness,
purifying alienation:
This is exactly what I came here for.
There is nothing more.

The snow brings silence with it,
sinking into the frozen darkness of a Sunday night.
On these tired, sour, leaden streets,
the bitter desolation is too much to take
for very long. I return to my station:
Stretched out on a bed,
gazing at a distant mountain range
or staring at a faucet in a trance.
It's not refreshing, it doesn't seem strange
and seductive, as it appeared in advance.
Far from the City of Refuge,
with no practical scheme,
constantly ruing the latest version
of what might have been, emptying myself
into the emptiness, negotiating the rush,
as a pick-up truck plows through the slush;
and I resign myself to another night, another day,
serving out a sentence.
I told myself I'd stay.

& Other Poems of Regret and Resentment

Outsiders here are quickly identified:
they're clean shaven.
I observe the bartender's warmth
with other customers.
Surrounded by laughter,
I watch the bubbles in my beer,
shooting from the bottom of the glass
to a rapidly nearing surface, evenly spaced,
like asteroids in a primitive video game,
and leave unthanked.
On the street a creature is drawn to me:
A vicious black dog, grudgingly restrained
by an unapologetic owner.
These excursions strike me now,
as they always strike me at this point,
as being selfish and pointless.
What am I doing here?
When will I learn?
Despite all the goodwill I brought with me,
the place gave me nothing in return.

ON THE ROAD AGAIN

It's all gone now, replaced by shadows
and simulacra, yet we cling to the dream.
Life passed through here once,
it could happen again.

A good humor man nurtures a roadside weed
with water from a Dixie Cup;
street lights change superfluously in muggy stillness;
in a world of blinding blandness,
a poisonous vacancy becomes beautiful.

Travel broadens the mind: It is refreshing
to sharpen familiar fears and sorrows in unfamiliar climes;
to commune with nature, with music, silently
with strangers; to throw my woes, without relief,
into relief, and resign myself, yet again,
to the decline of the West and the death of the quest,
before returning, empty-handed and heavy-lidded,
smoke streaming from a clenched fist in a rear view mirror,
to the stifling safety zone where I can continue
to sink unimpeded.

NEW MORNING, OLD AFTERNOON

I hate waking up
in the middle of the night, defenseless
against the sudden intrusion of reality.
To lie there facing stark uncertainties,
seeing things clearly in the darkness:
my conscience coming to light, blooming
like a poisonous night flower. Waiting
to become less aware, to disappear,
as gradually the starkness smooths out and slips away.
It was, after all, only a small concession to reality.
In the morning it will be forgotten.

Like a cat stretched out in the sun,
I don't need anyone
to need me, just someone to feed me.
I don't need a mountain
named after me, don't need a legacy.
The world at large is a faraway place.
I am on nodding off terms with reality,
and I am complete enough in myself to do nothing
but watch shadows drift across a wall,
and a circle of light quivering upon the floor.

HEROIC LIVING

We sit around talking about men who were greater than us:
the chosen ones, the ones who chose themselves, whom we chose
over ourselves; the ones who did the work that we
are incapable of doing. Separated from greatness by talent,
determination and fame, we utter their talismanic names,
basking briefly in the hazily reflected glory of their charmed lives,
before returning, briefly emboldened, to trying to survive.

We once imagined that our movements would be similarly traced.
But that was a long time ago,
and nothing has happened since then.
Our words have gone unweighed, our stations unsurveyed,
because we weren't driven or desperate enough,
and because we didn't know the right people. Now we are never
going to be filmed in slow motion; never going to be approached
by a stranger and told that we are great;
never going to be overawed at being over-rewarded
for simply performing our task;
corrupted by flattery, sapped by wealth,
the clawing at the void behind the mask.

And despite their peerless brilliance,
our bon mots will never be disseminated.

Neither will our graciousness be reported on.

None of this, not retrospectively, or even posthumously.
For to fail modestly is a sad possibility, and to remain modest,
under the circumstances, sadly impossible.
We talk about 'the work.' But, unfortunately,
there is nobody of sufficient worth
to recognize our worth.

& Other Poems of Regret and Resentment

Perhaps it was understood,
even at the time, that it was just a phase,
a rite of passage, not a way of life;
one was proceeding in precisely the right direction:
It was one's duty to act as if one were immortal
until otherwise notified. And perhaps,
upon mature consideration, one privately accepted
that the overstatement of one's reaction
was equal to one's lack of conviction;
that one only had so much time in which to cultivate
a credibility that could be lived off for years:
to sink as low as possible
before picking oneself up
and 'moving on.'

Perhaps one was aware, all along,
that practicality would eventually triumph
over frivolous excess,
that a more sensible and satisfying journey
lay beyond this vicarious precariousness:
the hallowed passage of becoming desperate enough
to change, to seek compensation for being oneself,
and to provide, both genetically and industriously,
for one's posterity.

Well, it was fun while it lasted:
'A struggle,' as you now call it.
You had the time of your life
and you got to act like a martyr about it.
But on to more serious concerns,
without pathological or chemical excuse:
simmer down, flatten out, enjoy the good things in life.
Renounce your virtues and reproduce.

Acknowledgments

Many of these poems have appeared in magazines, mostly in the pages of *Artillery* —

Additionally: *Southern Humanities Review, Slake, Forth, Dialectical Anthropology* and *Paris, LA.*